KNOW YOUR SCIENCE TOOLS

LET'S USE A THERMOMETER

DENNIS LIU

PowerKiDS press

Published in 2027 by The Rosen Publishing Group, Inc.
2544 Clinton Street, Buffalo, NY 14224

First Edition

Editor: Noah Riccardi
Book Design: Claire Vanden Branden

Photo Credits: Cover, p. 1 Suranto W./Shutterstock.com; p. 5 Javier Volcan/Shutterstock.com; p. 7 Denis Prokofev/Shutterstock.com; p. 9 Dmitry Naumov/Shutterstock.com; p. 11 R. Villalon/Shutterstock.com; p. 13 Josie Elias/Shutterstock.com; p. 15 D. C. Studio/Shutterstock.com; p. 17 RidgebackStudio/Shutterstock.com; p. 19 Mr. PK/Shutterstock.com; p. 21 alicancomertpay/Shutterstock.com.

Cataloging-in-Publication Data
Names: Liu, Dennis.
Title: Let's use a thermometer / Dennis Liu.
Description: Buffalo, New York : PowerKids Press, 2027. | Series: Know your science tools | Includes glossary and index.
Identifiers: ISBN 9781499459609 (pbk.) | ISBN 9781499459616 (library bound) | ISBN 9781499459623 (ebook)
Subjects: LCSH: Thermometers--Juvenile literature.
Classification: LCC QC271.4 L58 2027 | DDC 536.50287--dc23

Manufactured in China

CPSIA Compliance Information: Batch #QS27PK. For Further Information contact Rosen Publishing, at 1-800-237-9932.

CONTENTS

How Hot Is Hot?

Let's make some candy! If you heat the candy mix to a certain **temperature**, it'll be soft when cool. If you heat it to a higher temperature, it'll become hard. But how hot exactly does the candy mix become? A thermometer can tell us the answer.

5

Hot and Cold

Thermometers are tools people use to tell temperature. We use them in a lot of ways. You might check a thermometer to find out the temperature outdoors. People use thermometers when cooking to make sure food is safe to eat.

The thermometer shown on page 9 is a liquid-in-glass thermometer. It uses a special liquid that changes with temperature. As temperatures rise, the liquid in a thermometer warms up. The liquid expands and takes up more space. That's why the liquid rises in the tube. When the temperature falls, the liquid takes up less space and falls in the tube.

0
10
20

Taking the Temperature

Thermometers may show two kinds of **units**: Celsius and Fahrenheit. People in the United States often use Fahrenheit (F), but most other countries use Celsius (C) units. For example, the temperature at which water freezes is 0° in Celsius and 32° in Fahrenheit.

°C
°F
50
40
30
20
10
120
100
80
60
40

When you take the temperature from a liquid-in-glass thermometer, the thermometer should be upright. Your eyes should be even with the top of the liquid. The number next to the liquid's highest point is the temperature.

F
C
50
40
30
20
10
0
70
50
40

Know This Science Tool

Doctors use thermometers a lot. It can be important to know the temperature of a body. The temperature reading can tell us if we're ill. Many thermometers are **digital** so they're easier to read.

Some thermometers can tell temperature at a large distance. **Infrared** thermometers use **lenses** to help measure surface temperature. **Astronomers** use these thermometers to find out temperatures on planets very far from Earth!

°C/°F
Emis.
Mode
Lock
°C

Sometimes scientists need to measure very hot or cold temperatures. They use special tools in these cases. They might not look much like thermometers! Resistance thermometers use **electricity** to measure temperature. They're very exact, and they can measure temperatures of more than 1,500°F (816°C)!

Scientists are always making new and better kinds of thermometers. One kind is so small you can't even see it. It can measure the temperature inside a **cell**! It might be used to fight illnesses someday. Why do you use thermometers?

GLOSSARY

astronomers: Scientists who study space.

cell: The smallest basic part of a living thing.

digital: Showing numbers rather than using a pointer or marker that must be read.

electricity: A form of energy that goes through wires and powers machines.

infrared: A kind of invisible light whose waves are longer than those that make red light.

lenses: Clear, curved pieces of glass or plastic that change the direction of light rays.

temperature: How hot or cold something is.

units: Amounts of length, weight, volume, or other measurements.

FOR MORE INFORMATION

BOOKS

Harts, Marie. *Measurement*. Buffalo, NY: Rosen Publishing, 2024.

O'Daly, Anne. *Measuring Temperature*. Buffalo, NY: Rosen Publishing, 2024.

WEBSITES

BBC Bitesize: Measuring: Temperature
bbc.co.uk/teach/skillswise/articles/zh4ghbk
Learn more about how to read temperatures at this site.

Britannica Kids: Temperature
kids.britannica.com/students/article/temperature/313807
Learn more about the study of temperature here.

INDEX